East Sussex
County Council

eastsussex.gov.uk

East Sussex Library and Information Services
~~Schools Library and Museum Service~~

First published in the UK in 2015 by

Ivy Press

210 High Street

Lewes

East Sussex BN7 2NS

United Kingdom

www.ivypress.co.uk

British Library Cataloguing-in-Publication Data
A catalogue record for this book is available from the British Library

ISBN: 978-1-78240-237-4

This book was conceived, designed and produced by

Ivy Press

CREATIVE DIRECTOR Peter Bridgewater
PUBLISHER Susan Kelly
COMMISSIONING EDITOR Hazel Songhurst
PROJECT EDITOR Polly Goodman
ART DIRECTOR Kim Hankinson
DESIGNER Emily Portnoi
ILLUSTRATORS
Melvyn Evans (colour)
Marta Munoz (black and white)

Printed in China

Colour origination by Ivy Press Reprographics

10 9 8 7 6 5 4 3 2 1

Distributed worldwide (except North America) by Thames & Hudson Ltd,
181A High Holborn, London WC1V 7QX, United Kingdom

Ancient Egypt
IN 30 SECONDS

CATH SENKER

ILLUSTRATED BY MELVYN EVANS
CONSULTANT: DR JACQUELYN WILLIAMSON

Ivy Kids

Contents

Awesome Ancient Egypt
. . . in 60 seconds

What do you already know about Ancient Egypt? You've probably heard of the pyramids? And the mummies, too? In fact we know an amazing amount about the Ancient Egyptians. For example, we know that they liked to wear make-up, to dance at religious ceremonies, to hunt lions and to eat fish from the River Nile. How do we know these things? After all, the Ancient Egyptians lived 5,000 years ago. We know because they left behind so many things that tell us about their lives.

Archaeologists have found fantastic paintings that show us what they looked like, how they dressed and how they spent their time. Lots of artefacts such as statues, pottery and jewellery have also been discovered. The Ancient Egyptians' writing language has been decoded by scholars so we can now understand what they wrote about.

And this takes us back to the preserved bodies of the dead, known as mummies, and the great stone tombs, called pyramids. The mummies and pyramids preserved the remains of people and all the goods that were buried with them – from pots to intricate jewellery. This is how we know so much about the Ancient Egyptians.

This book uncovers some of the fascinating details of Egyptian life. Find out about their jobs – who did the tough work and who had it easy? Was the food tasty? How did people stay cool in the scorching hot weather? And what did they do for entertainment in those days long before books, TV and the Internet? All these questions and more are answered here.

Every topic has a page to read in 30 seconds for a quick grasp of the facts. If you are in a real hurry you can read the speedy 3-second sum-up instead. Each full-page illustration supplies a colourful at-a-glance guide, too. Then, if you have a spare few minutes, there are extra facts to discover and exciting hands-on activities to try.

The Ancient Egyptians

By around 5000 BCE, people living along the River Nile had started to farm the land. They grew wheat and barley crops, and raised cattle. By 3500 BCE, a few cities had developed and people started to invent writing. A sophisticated and well-organized civilization grew up. In around 3000 BCE, King Menes united the country of Ancient Egypt. He ruled with the help of trusted advisors, religious leaders and highly educated scribes.

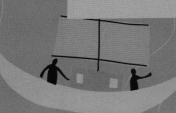

The Ancient Egyptians
Glossary

archaeologist A person who studies the cultures of the past by examining the remains of buildings and objects found in the ground.

Bedouin An Arab people that traditionally live in the desert.

civilization A state of human society that is very developed and organized.

desert A large area of land that has very little water and very few plants growing on it.

fertile Land where plants grow well.

flood A large amount of water covering an area that is usually dry.

invader An army that enters another country by force in order to take control of it – this is called an invasion.

linen A type of cloth made from the flax plant. The Egyptians used linen to make clothing. We still use linen today.

locust A large, winged insect that lives in hot countries and flies in big groups, eating all the plants and crops in an area.

monument A statue or building constructed to remind people of a famous person or event.

noble Belonging to a family that is very important in society.

pharaoh The ruler of Ancient Egypt. The ordinary people believed that he or she was a god on earth.

pyramid A giant tomb built for the pharaohs of Egypt. It was made from stone with a square base and four sloping sides that came to a point at the top.

relief A scene carved out of stone, wood or other material.

ritual A series of actions that are always performed in the same way as part of a religious act.

scribe An important person in Ancient Egypt who was trained to write and helped to run the country.

tax In Ancient Egypt, a part of people's farm produce that they had to pay to the government each year.

temple In Ancient Egypt, a building used for the worship of gods and goddesses.

unite To bring together to form a whole. For example, Lower and Upper Egypt were brought together to form one whole country.

warrior A person who fights in a battle. A soldier.

A rich civilization
... in 30 seconds

By 3000 BCE, the rich and powerful civilization of Ancient Egypt had developed by the banks of the River Nile in northeast Africa. It had a capital city with beautiful temples. People lived in mud-brick homes and grew fruit and vegetables. The wealthy lived in luxury. The soil was fertile and farmers grew plentiful food crops.

This great civilization traded goods with distant lands. Skilled craftworkers created elaborate furniture, beautiful pottery, intricate jewellery and linen clothing. A complex writing system developed. Highly educated scribes, who helped run the country, kept records of important decisions and events. Religious beliefs inspired the construction of monumental buildings.

Ancient Egypt was cut off from other lands by the sea and a vast expanse of desert so it was hard for invaders to attack. This helped this amazing civilization survive for around 3,000 years.

3-second sum-up

Ancient Egyptian civilization flourished from 3000 BCE, and lasted for around 3,000 years.

Timeline

Ancient Egyptian history is divided into five different periods:

Around 3000 BCE: King Menes unites Upper Egypt in the south with Lower Egypt in the north.
Old Kingdom (2575–2130 BCE): The pyramids were built.
Middle Kingdom (about 1938–1630 BCE): Egypt conquered Nubia (now Sudan).
New Kingdom (about 1539–1075 BCE): Egypt was at its most powerful and wealthy.
The Late Period (from 1075–30 BCE): Egypt's power declined.

Ancient Egypt was a rich civilization that grew up along the banks of the River Nile around 5,000 years ago.

The River Nile runs right through Egypt.

The Egyptians buried their kings inside giant pyramids.

Farmers grew crops on the river banks.

Traders transported goods by land and sea.

Craftworkers made pottery, jewellery and linen cloth.

Scribes kept records.

The River Nile

... in 30 seconds

Water from the River Nile was vital to the Ancient Egyptians. It was used for farming, drinking and washing. It also supplied fish to eat, and was a perfect route for moving goods and people up and down the land. Without it, the civilization could not have developed.

The Egyptians called the area beside the Nile the Black Land because each year, the river flooded and dumped fertile black mud over the land. Beyond lay the Red Land – the hot, sandy desert. Only the Bedouin people lived in the open desert, enduring the lack of rain and the harsh sun.

The River Nile created three seasons:
Flood season: While the river flooded the land, no one could farm. They worked on building projects instead.
Ploughing season: When the water drained away, farmers sowed their crops.
Harvest season: Farmers cut and stored the crops. They had to pay part of the harvest to the pharaoh as tax. It was bad luck if locusts had munched most of your crops – you still had to pay up.

3-second sum-up

The Ancient Egyptians depended on the River Nile for water, food and transport.

3-minute mission Make a flood

You need: • Paper • Baking tray with sides • Modelling clay

1 Sketch a river, 2.5 cm (1 inch) wide and the length of a baking tray. Draw streams flowing into the top third of the river.

2 Build a clay model of your river sketch in the baking tray, with riverbanks 1 cm (⅓ inch) high.

3 Pour water into the river. Tip the model slightly at the end. Add more water and see what happens!

Ancient Egyptian life was based around the River Nile. Every year it flooded, leaving fertile mud on its land.

During the flood season, farmers helped to construct the pyramids and other important buildings.

In the ploughing season, farmers sowed their crops in the damp, fertile soil.

During the harvest season, the crops were cut and stored. The stalks were used to make mats and baskets.

The pharaohs

... in 30 seconds

The ruler of Ancient Egypt was the pharaoh. He (or she) lived in luxury in a huge palace and owned all of the land. The pharaoh was responsible for the welfare of their people, who believed they were a junior god on earth. The pharaohs ruled peacefully most of the time.

The first pharaoh was King Menes, in about 3000 BCE. Menes united Lower and Upper Egypt as one country, and built the capital city of Memphis. You can still see its ruins today.

In about 2600 BCE, the pharaoh Djoser built Egypt's first pyramid, called the Step Pyramid. It had six platforms and was 62 m (204 ft) high. It was the first important stone building ever built in Egypt.

Pharaoh Khufu constructed the biggest pyramid of all in about 2589 BCE – the Great Pyramid at Giza. As well as his fame in battles, the warrior pharaoh Ramesses the Great, who ruled in the 1200s BCE, built a huge number of monuments.

3-second sum-up

The kings of Ancient Egypt were called pharaohs and were believed to be gods.

World famous

The boy-king Tutankhamun wasn't an important pharaoh but he is definitely the most famous. Archaeologist Howard Carter discovered his tomb in the Valley of the Kings in 1922. It was the only one that hadn't been robbed, so his mummy with its golden death mask, jewellery, weapons, furniture and clothes were still intact. This amazing discovery captured the world's imagination and gave us a wealth of information about Ancient Egypt.

Thousands of years ago, Egypt was ruled by powerful kings called pharaohs.

The first pharaoh, Menes, built Memphis, the biggest city in the ancient world.

Menes united Upper and Lower Egypt into one country.

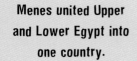

Lower Egypt

Upper Egypt

3000 BCE

Djoser built Egypt's first pyramid – the Step Pyramid.

2600 BCE

The Great Pyramid at Giza was built by Khufu.

2589 BCE

Ramesses the Great led his troops into battle to regain lost Egyptian lands.

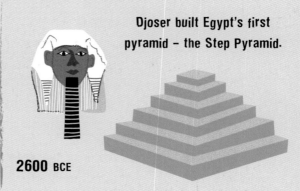

1300 BCE

Female pharaohs

... in 30 seconds

Most of the high officials in Ancient Egypt were men, but women also could hold senior posts, and some became pharaohs. Sobekneferu is the first known female pharaoh. She ruled for nearly four years in the 1790s BCE. We know little about her reign.

In the 15th century BCE, the daughter of Pharaoh Thutmose, Hatshepsut, became pharaoh. At first, she ruled on behalf of her young stepson, Thutmose III, but after a few years, she made herself pharaoh.

Hatshepsut adopted a ceremonial headdress and false beard to look like a proper pharaoh. She built a splendid temple near Thebes, with reliefs listing the important events of her reign.

Cleopatra became the last pharaoh of Egypt in 51 BCE. Her father wanted Cleopatra and her brother to be joint rulers, but her brother decided to rule alone and forced her out of Egypt. Cleopatra, however, was determined to be pharaoh, and with the help of the Roman leader Julius Caesar, she regained the throne.

3-second sum-up

Women were able to hold important jobs, including the top job of pharaoh.

Women in Ancient Egypt

Ancient Egypt was probably the best place to be a woman in ancient times. Women had more rights than in other lands. They could buy property and become traders, and the laws treated them the same as men. Rich noblewomen stayed at home and ran large households. Poorer women went out to work and did all kinds of jobs alongside men.

Though most pharaohs were men, a few women were able to rule Egypt successfully.

Hatshepsut was sure that her father had wanted her to become pharaoh after him.

She wore a headdress and a false beard so she would be seen as a proper pharaoh.

Hatshepsut strengthened the Egyptian economy. Her greatest monument was Deir el-Bahri.

Female Pharaohs Hall of Fame

SOBEKNEFERU
About 1799–1795 BCE

HATSHEPSUT
About 1473–1458 BCE

TAUSERT
About 1193–1190 BCE

CLEOPATRA
About 51–30 BCE

Egyptian society

... in 30 seconds

Egyptian society was organized just like a pyramid, with the pharaoh at the top and a mass of labourers and servants at the bottom.

The pharaoh reigned over Egypt, but didn't have time to run the whole country without help. The vizier (chief advisor) took charge – rather like a prime minister. Below the vizier were the district governors, with each governor ruling one of the 42 regions of Egypt.

The pharaoh was head of religion, too, but the priests and priestesses ran the temples, performing the daily rituals and organizing the festivals. Priests also helped run the country, and often became trusted advisors to the pharaoh.

Scribes were also of noble rank. They were highly educated, extremely important and helped to run the country. Egyptian society could not operate without them.

Builders and craftspeople made useful products, and some even rose to become nobles. Then there were the traders, shopkeepers and farmers. Labourers did the dirty and dangerous jobs – lugging stones or digging in the mines. People often did this kind of work as a way of paying their taxes.

3-second sum-up

Educated people were at the top of Egyptian society and the uneducated at the bottom.

3-minute mission Position wanted!

If you lived in Ancient Egypt, which job would you like? A priest or priestess in charge of a temple, an important scribe helping to run the country by recording important data, or a skilled craftworker? Imagine you are looking for work. Write a letter to the pharaoh listing your skills and explaining why you would be the perfect person for the job.

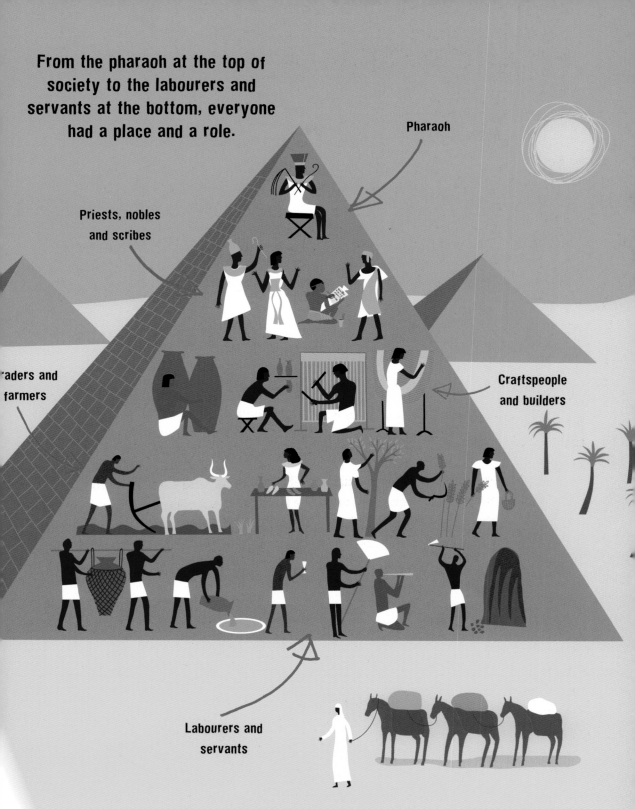

From the pharaoh at the top of society to the labourers and servants at the bottom, everyone had a place and a role.

Pharaoh

Priests, nobles and scribes

Traders and farmers

Craftspeople and builders

Labourers and servants

At home

We know a lot about everyday life from paintings and other artefacts left by the Ancient Egyptians. Their pictures of banquets show us their favourite foods, and the outfits, jewellery and make-up they liked to wear. Information has also come from archaeologists, who have found household goods, food, clothes and furniture from the tombs of wealthy Egyptians.

At home
Glossary

acacia A tree with yellow or white flowers.

anklet A piece of jewellery, like a bracelet, worn around the ankle.

barley A plant grown for its grain that the Ancient Egyptians also used for making beer.

cloak A coat without sleeves that fastens at the neck and hangs loosely from the shoulders, worn in cold weather in Ancient Egypt.

henna A reddish-brown dye used to change the colour of hair and skin.

imported Brought in or introduced from another country.

intruder A person who enters a building or an area without having permission.

kilt A short skirt with pleats (folds in the cloth).

linen A type of cloth made from the flax plant. The Egyptians used linen to make clothing. We still use linen today.

loincloth A piece of cloth worn around the body at the hips by some men in Ancient Egypt.

lotus A plant with white or pink flowers that grows on the surface of lakes in Africa and Asia.

pickled Preserving food to make it keep longer by storing it in vinegar or salt water.

pleat A long, narrow fold in a piece of clothing.

preserve To stop food or a body from rotting.

robe A long, loose outer piece of clothing.

scorpion A small creature, with eight legs, two front claws and a long tail that curves over its back that can give a poisonous sting. It lives in hot countries.

smoked Preserving food, especially meat and fish, so it keeps longer, using smoke from a burning material such as wood.

tunic A loose piece of clothing covering the body down to the knees, usually without sleeves.

wax A solid substance made by bees, which becomes soft when heated.

wick In Ancient Egypt, a twisted length of linen or natural fibre in the middle of a bowl of oil that was lit to make a small flame.

Living space

... in 30 seconds

In Ancient Egypt, the weather was scorching hot for much of the year. To stay cool, the Egyptians built their houses with small, high windows, which kept out the sun. They often painted the outside walls white to reflect the heat. Sometimes they built homes on raised platforms to protect them from flooding.

Wealthy people had large homes with plenty of well-furnished rooms. They relaxed in gardens, with fig and acacia trees providing shade, and beautiful pools filled with fish and lotus flowers.

Most Egyptians had simple furniture, such as beds, stools, a low table carved from wood and, maybe, a few brick benches. They stored their clothes in chests or baskets.

When it grew dark, people lit a wick in a bowl of oil. It wouldn't have given out much light though, so it is probable that people went to bed soon after dusk. They slept on beds made from a wooden frame raised on bricks. For a pillow, they used a hard stone or a wooden headrest – which doesn't sound very comfortable!

3-second sum-up

Rich people had large, comfortable homes, while the poor lived simply with little furniture.

Interior design

Wealthy Egyptians loved to decorate their homes. They painted the walls and floors with pretty patterns, or pictures of birds, animals and plants. Sometimes, they used wall hangings and brightened up the floor with coloured tiles. Pharaohs had images of their enemies painted on their floors so they could stamp on them.

Most homes were made of mud bricks but wealthy people had much larger houses.

In summer, people slept on the flat roof to keep cool.

Even wealthy homes were built with bricks made of mud from the River Nile.

There were high walls around the home to keep out intruders.

People ate, played and relaxed in the garden around the pool.

Food and drink

... in 30 seconds

If you were an Ancient Egyptian, you'd mostly survive on bread and barley beer. Your diet would be livened up with fresh fruit, vegetables and fish, so it would be fairly healthy. You would also eat foods that you'd dried, salted, smoked or pickled to preserve them.

The Egyptians were the first people to use yeast to make bread rise, but unfortunately their bread was horrible. When they ground the flour between two stones, bits of grit were left in the flour. The bread was so rough and gritty that it wore down people's teeth!

People drank beer because it tasted better than water from the Nile, which was often quite brown and dirty. The alcohol killed the germs, too. But the beer was rough stuff. You had to drink it using a tube so you didn't choke on lumps of mashed barley.

The rich spoiled themselves with tasty treats. They feasted on all kinds of meat, from beef, mutton and pork to exotic ostrich, antelope and pelican. Wealthy people enjoyed desserts, which were sweetened with honey because sugar didn't exist. They washed down their dinner with expensive wine imported from Syria and Palestine.

3-second sum-up

People had a mostly healthy diet that included fresh fish, fruit and vegetables.

3-minute mission Egyptian treats

You need: • 12 pitted dates • Walnut pieces • 2 tablespoons of honey • 2 pinches of cinnamon • Ground almonds

1 Mix the honey and cinnamon in a bowl.
2 Stuff each date with walnut pieces.
3 Dip the dates in the cinnamon honey, then roll in ground almonds.

Bread was a basic part of the Ancient Egyptians' diet. This is how they made it.

1. People trampled the grain to make flour.

2. They mixed the grain with water and yeast to make dough.

3. They formed the dough into loaves, including animal shapes.

4. The loaves were baked in the oven.

5. Freshly baked bread!

Unfortunately the gritty bread was hard to chew!

Cool outfits

... in 30 seconds

Most Ancient Egyptians wore nothing at all. Workers often found it practical to go naked, especially if they were doing something like washing clothes in water. Young children walked around nude until they were about six – they could easily be washed after playing and there were no clothes to wash.

When people did wear clothes, they dressed in light, loose clothing to keep them cool. Working men usually wore a loincloth, while the wealthy dressed in kilts, tunics or robes, with cloaks when it was chilly. Women wore a long, straight dress, held on with one or two shoulder straps. Neither men nor women wore underwear.

Most clothing was made from linen, which comes from the flax plant. Rich people's garments were made from soft, finely woven linen. The poor made do with cheap, coarse cloth that must have been itchy against their skin.

Clothing was usually plain, without any buttons or zips. Garments were wrapped around the body and tied on, or fixed with a belt. Some rich people wore garments decorated with neat pleats, but no one knows how they made the pleats.

3-second sum-up

Clothing was designed to keep people cool and made from cotton or linen.

3-minute mission Sandal style

People in Ancient Egypt went barefoot most of the time. They only wore sandals for special occasions, or to protect their feet from snakes or scorpions. Look in books or online at the materials Ancient Egyptian sandals were made from. Which materials could you use today to make similar sandals?

Dressing up

... in 30 seconds

Everyone loved to dress up for a party! Wealthy people would wear their finest white linen dress or tunic. The linen was so fine it was see-through. They would add a brightly coloured beaded collar to their clothes and as much jewellery as they could afford.

Men and women wore rings, bracelets, anklets and ear studs – they pierced their ears just like people do today. The rich had gold jewellery, and many people wore fake versions made from a kind of pottery, called faience.

Make-up was regularly worn by the wealthy. Thick black eyeliner called kohl was especially popular. It helped reduce the glare from the Egyptian sun and ward off flies. People reddened their cheeks and lips with make-up made from iron oxide.

Wigs were essential party wear, too. Headlice were a common nuisance, so people tended to shave their heads or have very short hair. To dress up, they wore wigs made from human hair, held in place on their heads with sweet-smelling wax. As the party warmed up, the wax dripped down the wig, releasing a pleasant smell.

3-second sum-up

The wealthy dressed in wigs, jewellery and make-up for special occasions.

3-minute mission Design a party collar

Imagine the pharaoh has invited you to a party at his palace. Decide what you will wear and design a fabulous collar to go with your outfit. You could make one using thick card and decorate it with paint, coloured straws and sequins.

On special occasions, wealthy Egyptians
livened up their outfits with bright
collars and jewellery.

They fixed their wigs
in place with beeswax.

Both men and women
wore make-up.

They coloured their nails
and feet with henna.

They wore bangles made
from gold, silver and
precious stones.

Making a living

There were many ways of making a living in Ancient Egypt. Farmers looked after their animals, ploughed the soil, sowed seed and harvested the crops. Craftworkers made statues, pottery, sandals and elaborate jewellery. Builders constructed both grand and humble buildings. Some people worked as servants to the wealthy, others as labourers. One of the better jobs was to be a scribe, helping to run the kingdom.

Making a living
Glossary

antibiotic A substance that can stop the growth of bacteria (germs) and cure disease.

apprentice A young person who works for a skilled worker for a fixed period of time in order to learn the skills needed in a job.

artefact A handmade object, especially something of historical interest.

canal In Ancient Egypt, a long straight passage dug in the ground and filled with water to carry water to the fields.

civil servant A person who works for the government, helping to run the country.

civilization A state of human society that is very developed and organized.

climate The usual pattern of the weather in an area.

demotic The later form of hieratic writing with joined up characters.

desert A large area of land that has very little water and very few plants growing on it.

fertile Land where plants grow well.

granary A building for storing crops.

hieratic A quicker form of writing than hieroglyphic writing.

hieroglyph A picture or symbol of an object that stood for a word or sound in the Ancient Egyptian writing system.

invader When talking about the human body, something that attacks the cells, and which the body has to fight off.

irrigate To water.

linen A type of cloth made from the flax plant. The Egyptians used linen to make clothing. We still use linen today.

massage To rub and press a person's body to reduce pain.

mining Digging under the ground to find minerals, such as gold and iron.

official Someone who has a job in the government and can tell people what to do.

ox (plural: oxen) A large cow that is used to pull farm equipment.

papyrus Paper made from the stems of the papyrus plant, used in Ancient Egypt for writing and drawing on.

plaster A substance that is put on walls and ceilings to give them a smooth, hard surface.

pyramid A giant tomb built for the pharaohs of Egypt. It was made from stone with a square base and four sloping sides that came to a point at the top.

quarry A place where large amounts of stone are dug out of the ground.

reservoir A lake where water is stored.

ritual A series of actions that are always performed in the same way as part of a religious act.

scribe An important person in Ancient Egypt who was trained to write and helped to run the country.

sculptor A person who makes works of art by carving or shaping wood, stone or other materials.

shaduf A tool with poles, a rope, bucket and weight, used to raise water from canals for watering crops.

tomb A large grave, especially one built of stone above or below the ground.

worship In Ancient Egypt, showing respect for the gods by carrying out rituals, such as chanting hymns (songs of praise).

Farming

... in 30 seconds

Most Ancient Egyptians were farmers, working the fertile lands by the River Nile. They grew crops for food, and flax to make linen.

The Egyptians planted onions, garlic, cabbages and beans. Fruit such as melons, dates and pomegranates also grew well in the hot climate. Farmers kept cattle, pigs and sheep to provide meat, and geese for their eggs.

Farm tools were simple – hoes for weeding, sickles for cutting the crops and ploughs for turning the soil. Farmers often used oxen to pull ploughs.

The Egyptians built reservoirs and canals to store flood water for irrigation. They used a shaduf to raise water from the canals. This was a long pole attached to a cross-beam, with a rope and bucket at one end and a heavy weight at the other. The farmer lowered the bucket into the canal and levered it up by pulling down on the weight.

3-second sum-up

Farming was vital to the Egyptians and provided them with meat, grains, vegetables and fruits.

3-minute mission Make a shaduf

You need: • 4 thin sticks each 20 cm (8 inches) long • Play dough • Thread or string • A cup-cake case

1 Put a small blob of play dough on one end of three sticks. Stand them in a wigwam shape. Press the tops together with more play dough.

2 Tie the thread to one end of the fourth stick and press a play dough ball around the other end (this is the counterweight). Attach the cup-cake case (the bucket) to the other end of the thread.

3 Balance the stick on top of the wigwam, holding the play-dough ball.

Farmers grew crops, kept farm animals and irrigated their fields.

Oxen ploughed the fields and, at harvest time, they trampled the crop to separate the grain.

Farmers sowed crops such as wheat and barley once a year. They grew vegetables all year round.

They watered the growing crops by using a shaduf to fill buckets of water.

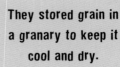

Farmers grew dates and other fruit such as pomegranates.

At harvest time, farmers cut down the crops with sickles – it was exhausting work.

They stored grain in a granary to keep it cool and dry.

Building and mining

... in 30 seconds

The Ancient Egyptians were great builders, well known for their extraordinary pyramids. Each pyramid took many years and thousands of workers to build.

Luckily, workers were not in short supply. The pharaohs knew that farmers could not work on the land while the Nile was flooding, so each year they got thousands of people to work on building projects instead.

Important buildings were made from stone, but most ordinary houses were made from simple mud bricks. Mud was readily available from the Nile. The bricks were quick to make, and if you decided you didn't want the house any more, you could knock it down and reuse some of the bricks. You could even abandon a palace if you didn't fancy it any more.

The Egyptians also made use of the land for mining. Precious stones and metals, such as gold, copper and iron, were found in the desert.

3-second sum-up

Most homes were made from mud bricks, but stone was used for special buildings.

3-minute mission Mini mud bricks

You need: • 1 mug mud • ⅔ mug water • Old bowl • Ice cube tray

1 Pour the mud into the bowl, add the water and mix.
2 Put the mud into the ice tray and press each one down with your thumb.
3 Leave the mud to dry overnight in a warm place.
4 Turn over the ice tray. You have made mud bricks. Now build a wall!

The Ancient Egyptians were skilled builders and miners.

Mud-brick houses were cool inside.

Vents in the roofs and walls allowed breezes to flow through.

Workers poured mud into wooden frames and left them to dry in the sun to form bricks.

The Egyptians used stone to build important buildings because they wanted them to last forever.

Prisoners and labourers were put to work as miners.

Creative craftspeople
... in 30 seconds

In around 1900 BCE an Ancient Egyptian scribe wrote, 'What can one say about the potter? He is still to be counted as a human being, but he digs about in the mud like a pig and his clothes are stiff with clay.'

This scribe was being incredibly rude. In fact, Egyptian craftspeople were highly skilled and produced beautiful paintings, sculptures, jewellery and other objects.

Craftspeople spent several years developing their skills. From about nine years old, boys learnt a craft from their parents, or became apprentices to experienced workers. Painters started off as scribes. If they had a talent for drawing, they trained as artists.

The Egyptians learned how to quarry stone and were extremely talented at building with it. Sculptors created elaborate stone figures of gods for worship, pounding and chipping away the stone. Craftspeople produced handy items for the home, too, such as pottery vessels.

3-second sum-up

Craftworkers made beautiful pottery vessels, stone sculptures and paintings.

3-minute mission Draw a tomb scene

You need: • Coarse sandpaper • Crayons

Egyptian artists painted elaborate scenes on sandy tomb walls. If you were an artist, what kind of scene would you like to draw? Use crayons to design and draw one on sandpaper. You could draw the bodies facing you and the heads turned to the side, just like the Ancient Egyptians.

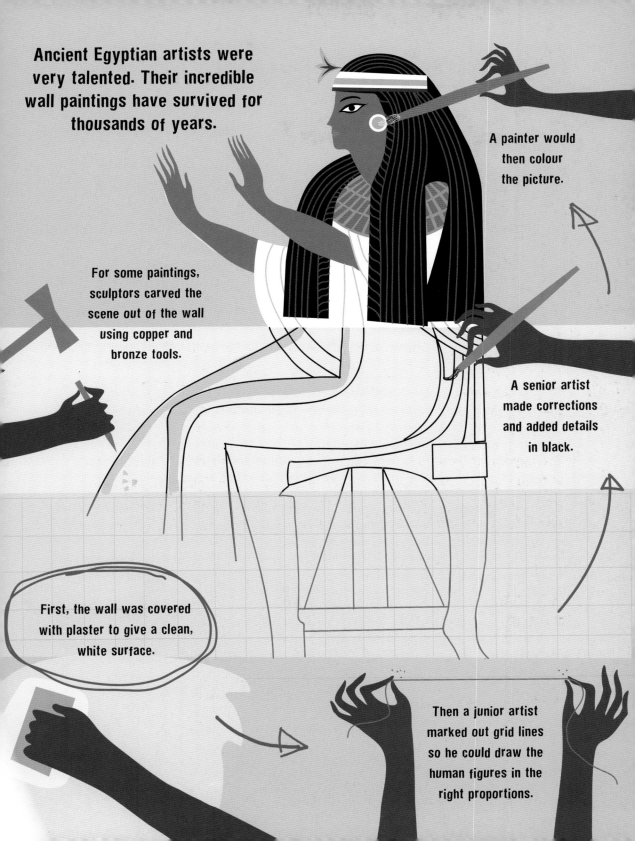

Ancient Egyptian artists were very talented. Their incredible wall paintings have survived for thousands of years.

A painter would then colour the picture.

For some paintings, sculptors carved the scene out of the wall using copper and bronze tools.

A senior artist made corrections and added details in black.

First, the wall was covered with plaster to give a clean, white surface.

Then a junior artist marked out grid lines so he could draw the human figures in the right proportions.

Superior scribes
... in 30 seconds

A few lucky Ancient Egyptian boys trained to be scribes. Being a scribe was a fantastic job because it didn't involve getting dusty and dirty, and it was less tiring than farming.

Student scribes spent seven years learning to read and write. They practised writing by copying out stories and lists of words on stones or wooden slates.

Trained scribes were like civil servants. They ran the country and kept records on papyrus, which was made from the reeds that grew along the banks of the River Nile. The longest-known papyrus scroll is the Great Harris Papyrus, which is 41 m (134 ft) long – nearly half the length of a football pitch.

If you wanted to send a letter, you had to pay a scribe to write it. To post it, you went to the River Nile and looked for a boat going in the right direction. For a small fee, a crew member would be happy to take your letter to its destination.

3-second sum-up

Scribes wrote down the important events of the kingdom.

3-minute mission Fruit ink

Scribes made ink from natural materials. Make yours from fruit.

You will need: 100 g (4 oz) blackberries or cherries • Strainer • Spoon • Bowl • ½ teaspoon vinegar • ½ teaspoon salt

Warning: Protect surfaces and clothes from stains!

1 Put the fruit into the strainer and place over the bowl.
2 Use the back of a spoon to press the juice through the strainer.
3 Add vinegar and salt to the juice and mix well.
4 Dip a wooden stirrer or stick into the mixture and get writing!

Writing was the job of the scribes. They didn't have paper – instead they used papyrus leaves.

Strips of papyrus were laid side by side with another layer placed on top.

The strips were flattened with a mallet.

The juice of the papyrus naturally turned the mat of strips into a sheet of flat paper.

To make a pen, scribes chewed the end of a reed to a point.

For red ink, they used reddish soil.

For black ink, they coloured blocks of gum with soot.

Writing

... in 30 seconds

What did those highly trained scribes spend so long learning to write? You've probably heard that the Egyptians wrote in hieroglyphs. They used this complicated form of writing for important documents.

Many hieroglyphs are like little pictures. That's because some signs stand for objects in daily life. For example, an eye with flowing tears means 'to weep'. Other signs stand for different sounds, such as the 'b' in boat or the 'sh' in show.

Hieroglyphs were usually written from right to left, but they could also be written from left to right and vertically. How can you tell how to read them? Signs showing animals or people look towards the start of the text. If the sign looks to the left, you read from left to right.

Ordinary people used a faster form of writing, called hieratic. This used simpler versions of the pictures so they were easier to write with a pen. Later on, the Egyptians used demotic writing and then Greek.

Most Ancient Egyptians could not read or write at all. They relied on word of mouth to find out what was happening in the world and good memories to remember the past.

3-second sum-up

The Ancient Egyptians wrote important documents in hieroglyphs.

3-minute mission Secret messages!

Why not write messages to your friends using hieroglyphs as a secret code? Try adding some new hieroglyphs for objects in your life, such as a mobile phone, computer game or skateboard.

Hieroglyphs used pictures to represent different letters, objects, actions or sounds.

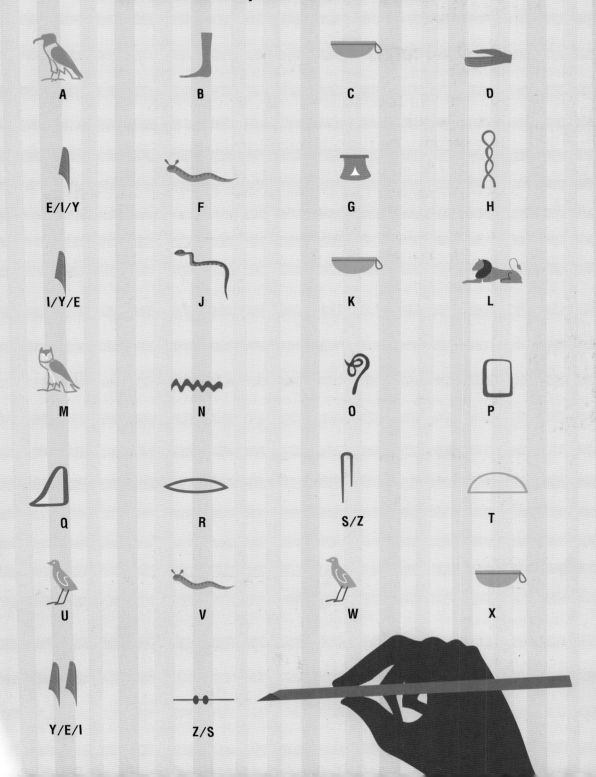

A

B

C

D

E/I/Y

F

G

H

I/Y/E

J

K

L

M

N

O

P

Q

R

S/Z

T

U

V

W

X

Y/E/I

Z/S

Healing the sick
... in 30 seconds

Ancient Egyptian healing was a fascinating mixture of medicine and magic. If you fell ill, you called the doctor to bring remedies and cast helpful spells.

The Egyptians were the first civilization to study medicine. A papyrus that dates back to the 16th century BCE lists 48 injuries and how to treat them. Doctors examined their patients carefully. They cleaned and stitched wounds, used splints for broken bones, and massage for aches and pains – all sensible treatments.

Yet the Egyptians were convinced that diseases came from evil spirits that invaded the body. They thought medicines helped the pain, but magic cured the illness. Magicians tried to drive out the spirits by muttering spells, carrying out strange rituals and inserting nasty substances such as poo into body openings to fight the invaders. One revolting treatment for toothache involved putting half a freshly killed mouse on the gum!

Often, the 'cures' made the poor patient even more ill. But although Egyptian medicine was rather hit or miss, there was nowhere else in the ancient world that you'd have found better doctors.

3-second sum-up

Some Ancient Egyptian cures worked, but others could be deadly.

Cured by chance

Some cures worked, even though it's unlikely the Egyptians understood the reasons why. For example, they put honey on wounds because they believed that evil spirits hated it. In fact, honey might have helped to heal cuts because it is an antibiotic. Doctors recommended munching raw garlic for colds, which we now know is helpful.

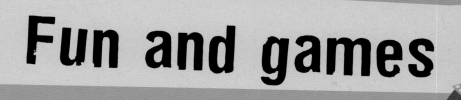

Fun and games

Pictures show that the Ancient Egyptians loved music, and played a variety of percussion, woodwind and stringed instruments. They enjoyed dancing displays, too. Outdoors, hunting and fishing were popular. Children also enjoyed games, and some of these games are similar to ones that children play today. Simple toys have been discovered, including little toy horses on wheels.

Fun and games
Glossary

afterlife The life that Ancient Egyptians believed that everyone had after death.

antelope An African or Asian animal, like a deer, that runs very fast.

chariot An open vehicle with two wheels, pulled by horses, and used in battles.

desert A large area of land that has very little water and very few plants growing on it.

enclosure A piece of land that is surrounded by a fence or wall and is used for a particular purpose.

game Wild animals that people hunt for sport or food.

gazelle A small antelope – an African or Asian animal, like a deer, that runs very fast.

javelin A light spear that is thrown in a sporting event or used as a weapon.

leapfrog A children's game in which players take turns to jump over the backs of other players who are bending down.

lyre An ancient musical instrument with strings fastened in a frame shaped like a U. It was played with the fingers.

oryx A large, fast-running antelope from Africa or Asia, with long, straight horns.

papyrus Paper made from the stems of the papyrus plant, used in Ancient Egypt for writing and drawing on.

profession A type of job that needs special training or skill.

temple In Ancient Egypt, a building used for the worship of gods and goddesses.

throw stick A simple tool that is thrown to hunt small animals.

tug of war A game in which two teams pull at opposite ends of a rope until one team drags the other over a line on the ground.

Playtime

... in 30 seconds

It was tough luck if you came from a poor family because you spent most of the time at work and didn't get much free time. The wealthy were luckier, and the children of wealthy families spent their days playing games.

Children loved physical games, such as leapfrog and tug of war. Girls were particularly fond of playing catch. To make it more exciting, they hurled the ball while on piggyback or leaping in the air.

Egyptian children also played with dolls, model animals and spinning tops made from wood. Little ones loved to pull along toy horses on wheels. Board games were particularly popular with adults, especially Mehen and Senet.

Senet, a game of good against evil, is still played today. Images on the squares of the board represent good or bad fortune – you have to avoid the dangers to safely reach the afterlife. To move along the board, sticks, which were decorated on one side, were thrown. The number of sticks that landed decorated side-up told you how many spaces to move.

3-second sum-up

Wealthy Egyptians had the leisure time to play lots of games.

3-minute mission Design a snake game

Mehen was an Ancient Egyptian board game with counters. The board was in a snake shape, and the aim was to get your counters to the snake's head and back again without being eaten. Design your own snake game, using counters and a dice, and try it out with your friends.

Egyptian children and adults loved playing games – some of which we still enjoy today.

Children played make-believe games with wooden dolls and toys.

The board game Mehen was like the game of Snakes and Ladders we play today.

People loved to tell scary ghost stories or funny tales about the gods.

Paintings show children playing catch on piggyback.

Hunting and fishing
... in 30 seconds

The Ancient Egyptians were one of the first cultures to hunt for entertainment as well as for food. They enjoyed sitting by the river with a fishing rod, waiting for Nile perch or catfish to bite.

They also hunted fish and birds in the papyrus bushes of the river banks, hurling a wooden throw stick as soon as they spotted movement.

Hunting big game was a more dangerous business. Lions were a nuisance because they trampled crops, so large hunting parties risked their lives to track them down.

For rich people, hunting was a popular sport. They headed into the desert with servants to chase bulls, gazelles, oryx and antelopes. In later times, they travelled in horse-drawn chariots, bringing dogs to chase the prey. Once cornered, the hunters fired their javelins, spears, and bows and arrows.

King Amenhotep III claimed that he killed 96 bulls on one trip, which makes him sound incredibly brave. Even if it were true, the pharaoh had been in no danger. Dogs would have herded the bulls into an enclosure so that King Amenhotep could shoot them from the safety of his chariot.

3-second sum-up

The Egyptians hunted for fun as well as for food.

3-minute mission Throw sticks

We know from wall paintings that Ancient Egyptians used throw sticks as hunting weapons. Find out more about them. What size and shape were they? How did they travel through the air? Can you name a throw stick belonging to another ancient culture?

Song and dance
... in 30 seconds

The Ancient Egyptians loved to party! At big religious festivals and celebrations, flutes and harps were played to the rhythm of drums and bells. Everyone sang and clapped, and dancing girls twirled.

The Egyptians had a variety of percussion, wind and stringed instruments. Drums, bells and rattles called sistra kept the beat, while flutes and trumpets played the tunes. Musicians plucked harps, lyres and lutes, and people sang along.

Being a musician was a profession in Ancient Egypt. Musicians played in the temples and royal household, and they played and danced at parties.

Although playing an instrument wasn't a hobby, it's likely that people used music to cheer themselves up while they worked. Farmers may have sung songs to the beat of rhythm sticks as they ploughed or hoed.

Unfortunately, the Egyptians didn't write down their music, so we have no idea how it sounded. But we can tell from the pictures of energetic dancing that it was probably loud, lively and rhythmic!

3-second sum-up

People would celebrate special occasions with music, singing and dancing.

Dance like an Egyptian!

Both men and women danced. They used slow, graceful steps and expressive moves similar to ballet dancing today. Other moves were more acrobatic – the dancers leapt around and did cartwheels, backbends and the splits. The dancers wore see-through robes or simply a bead or shell belt so their bodies could move freely.

Different types of music and dancing were an important part of life.

Tambourines kept the beat.

The pipe is one of the oldest instruments in the world.

The lute had two or three strings on a long neck.

Harps were often enormous – as tall as the player.

Dancing was often very energetic.

Religion and the afterlife

Religion was central to Ancient Egyptian culture, and the pharaohs built amazing temples to their gods and goddesses. Many of these solid stone structures have survived, showing us how people worshipped at the temples. We know about Ancient Egyptian burial customs from remains discovered in the depths of pyramids. But outside the temples, the everyday religious practices of ordinary people are a mystery.

Religion and the afterlife
Glossary

afterlife The life that Ancient Egyptians believed that everyone had after death.

amulet A piece of jewellery that the Ancient Egyptians wore because they thought it protected them from bad luck and illness.

ancestor A person in your family who lived a long time ago.

archaeologist A person who studies the cultures of the past by examining the remains of buildings and objects found in the ground.

canopic jar The Ancient Egyptians placed body organs in jars called canopic jars when they were making a mummy.

deity A god or goddess.

desert A large area of land that has very little water and very few plants growing on it.

embalmer Someone who prevents a dead body from rotting by treating it with special substances – the Ancient Egyptians used natron, a kind of salt.

fertility Being fertile – when people can have children, and when the land produces crops.

honour To show respect, for example, to a god or goddess.

linen A type of cloth made from the flax plant. The Egyptians used linen to make clothing. We still use linen today.

mummy The body of a person or animal that has been stopped from rotting by treating it with special substances and wrapping it in cloth.

obelisk A tall, pointed stone column with four sides.

preserve To stop a food or body from rotting.

purified Made clean for religious purposes, usually by washing.

pyramid A giant tomb built for the pharaohs of Egypt. It was made from stone, had a square base, and four sloping sides that came to a point at the top.

ritual A series of actions that are always performed in the same way as part of a religious act.

sarcophagus A stone coffin, often decorative and placed above ground.

shrine A place where people come to worship.

soul The spiritual part of a person, which the Ancient Egyptians believed lived on after death.

spatula A tool for mixing and spreading things.

sphinx An Ancient Egyptian stone statue with a human head and the body of a lion lying down.

temple In Ancient Egypt, a building used for the worship of gods and goddesses.

tomb A large grave, especially one built of stone above or below the ground.

underworld The place that Ancient Egyptians believed people had to pass through to reach the afterlife. The underworld was full of dangers, so people needed magic to pass safely through it.

wisdom The ability to make sensible decisions and give good advice.

worship In Ancient Egypt, showing respect for the gods by carrying out rituals, such as chanting hymns (songs of praise).

Gods and goddesses

... in 30 seconds

The Ancient Egyptians didn't have the scientific knowledge to understand how the world worked, so they explained it through religion.

The Egyptians believed that there was a constant struggle between order and chaos in the world. Only the gods and goddesses could keep order. They made sure the sun rose in the morning, the Nile flooded each year and the crops grew every season.

The gods and goddesses controlled people's lives. There were hundreds of gods, and they all had different jobs, so you needed to honour the right one. For example, women thanked Bastet and Tawret for the safe arrival of a baby.

It was the sun god Re who was considered to be the most important. The Egyptians were right to think that without the sun, they would not exist.

The gods varied over time. For example, the sun god Re was combined with Amun, the god of Thebes, and became known as Amun-Re.

3-second sum-up

The Ancient Egyptians believed that hundreds of gods controlled everything in their lives.

3-minute mission Which god or goddess?

Race a friend to find out:

Who was the goddess of joy and love?

Which goddess ate the sun god Re at the end of each day and gave birth to him at the beginning of the next?

Who was the god of writing and knowledge?

Which god had a pot belly and was shown with water plants?

BASTET the cat goddess and goddess of childbirth.

HORUS the falcon-headed god who protected pharaohs.

OSIRIS the king of the underworld and god of fertility.

ANUBIS the jackal who brought the dead to the afterlife.

Hundreds of gods and goddesses controlled every aspect of life. Here are some of the most important.

RE the sun god and creator of people.

THOTH the moon god and god of wisdom.

KHNUM the god who created human souls.

The temple
... in 30 seconds

To keep their country safe from harm, the pharaohs constructed enormous temples dedicated to the worship of the gods.

Egyptian temples were huge stone structures, built to last forever. Sphinxes guarded an avenue in front of the temple, and statues of the pharaoh adorned the gate. Tall, thin obelisks, carved with the names of pharaohs and messages to the gods, stood at the temple entrance, positioned at the point where the sun's first rays fell each morning.

The great temples were not like churches or mosques, where people gather to worship. They were the private home of a deity. The figure of the god was kept in a shrine in a dark room in the heart of the temple, and only priests were allowed to enter.

Ordinary people only caught a glimpse of the shrines of the gods when the statues were paraded at religious festivals. They worshipped models of the gods at a simple shrine at home, offering them prayers and gifts.

3-second sum-up

Priests carried out rituals at the temple. The ordinary people worshipped at home.

3-minute mission Make a water clock

Priests used a water clock to work out the right times for the rituals. Water dripped from a hole in the base of a container, taking one hour to drop between two marks.

You will need: Clear plastic cup • Safety pin • Water • Tall glass • Timer • Marker pen

1 Make a hole with the pin in the base of the cup.

2 Fill the cup with water and rest the cup on the top of the glass.

3 Time how long it takes to empty. Every five minutes, mark the level of the water on the outside of the cup with a marker pen.

The priest carried out
rituals at the temple to
keep the gods happy.

The priest entered
the temple.

He took the statue of
the god out of the
shrine, undressed and
purified it.

He dressed the god in
fresh linen and rubbed
it with holy oils.

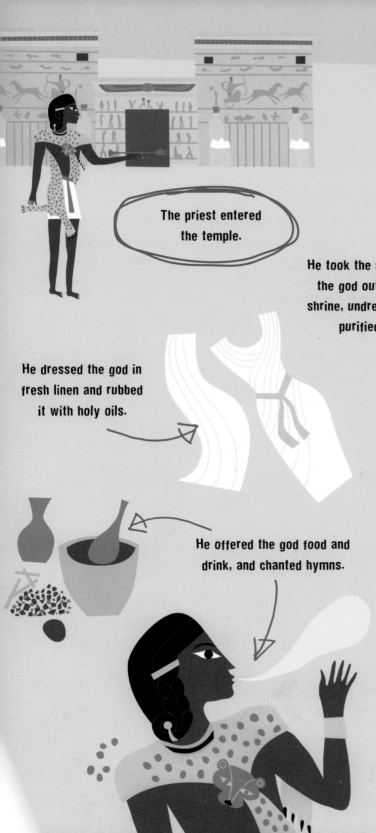

He offered the god food and
drink, and chanted hymns.

The priest put the statue
back in the shrine.

Festival time

... in 30 seconds

The Ancient Egyptians didn't have weekends and people worked every day, so religious festivals were extremely popular.

Festivals were a chance for people to celebrate their faith, take time off work and have some fun. The priests made offerings to the gods accompanied by loud music and energetic dancing in the streets.

Every year, the Festival of the Beautiful Embrace celebrated the marriage of the god Horus to the goddess Hathor. A statue of the goddess in a shrine was sailed by river from her temple at Dendera on a boat called the Mistress of Love. Upon arrival at Horus's temple in Edfu, Hathor was greeted by the falcon-headed Horus statue and a loud, lively crowd.

Opet was an important festival that took place during the flood season, lasting up to a month. It celebrated the pharaoh's rule as junior god on Earth. Statues of the gods Amun, Mut and Khonsu were brought from the temples at Karnak to the Luxor Temple on a 3-km (2-mile) procession. Priests, musicians, dancers, singers, soldiers and huge crowds accompanied the gods.

3-second sum-up

Religious festivals were lively and fun. People honoured the gods, sang and danced.

3-minute mission Celebrations

There are many different religious festivals, which are celebrated all through the year, all over the world. For example, on Diwali night, Hindus dress up in their best clothes, light lamps and pray to Lakshmi, the goddess of wealth and prosperity. Then there are fireworks, a family feast and presents. Do some research and find out about other religious festivals. Can you see any similarities between them?

Religious festivals were great celebrations and combined fun with worship.

During the Opet festival, the statue of the god Amun was carried in a sacred boat to the Luxor Temple.

Priests, musicians, dancers and large crowds welcomed Amun to Luxor.

Preserving bodies

... in 30 seconds

The Egyptians believed that when people died, their ka (soul) would live an afterlife in the underworld – a world rather like Egypt. So when a pharaoh or another important person died, the Egyptians didn't simply bury them in a grave. They preserved the body for its next life.

Cooks showed the embalmers what to do. They knew that to preserve meat you had to dry out the body and salt it. So the embalmers removed the gooey, wet organs: the liver, stomach, intestines and lungs and set them aside. They left the heart inside the body because they believed that's where the mind was. But they hooked out the brain through the nose and threw it away. The Egyptians didn't think the brain was important.

Next the embalmers covered the body with natron, a kind of salt that was good for drawing out liquids but left the body supple. They dried out the internal organs separately and placed them in their own containers, called canopic jars. The corpse rotted fast, so it was taken to the desert and left to dry out for 40 days.

3-second sum-up

The Ancient Egyptians believed in an afterlife and preserved the bodies of the dead so they could enjoy it.

3-minute mission The afterlife stash

As well as preserving their bodies, the Ancient Egyptians supplied a dead pharaoh with useful things like food as well as treasures like jewellery for their time in the underworld. If you were preparing a pharaoh for the afterlife what useful things and treasures from today's world do you think they would need? Make a list.

The Egyptians embalmed
bodies to preserve them
for the afterlife.

Then the embalmers broke
through the skull with a chisel.

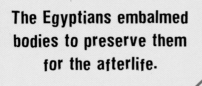

First, the embalmers
washed the body.

They used a piece of wire
with a hook on the end to
scoop the brain out.

They tied on the
fingernails and toe nails
so they didn't fall off.

They removed the internal
organs and put them in
four canopic jars.

The embalmers used natron to
pack the body and put it in a
tent for 40 days to dry out.

Making a mummy

... in 30 seconds

Once a pharaoh's dead body had dried out, it could be turned into a mummy. Without all the organs it was rather empty, so the embalmers stuffed it with linen or sawdust to make it look plump and lifelike.

If a finger or other body part had fallen off, the embalmers simply replaced it with a bit of wood. Then they wrapped up the body with linen bandaging, tucking in jewellery and amulets. Tutankhamun was buried with more than 150 pieces of jewellery!

Everything the mummy would need in the afterlife was prepared, including food, drink and household goods. There was a Book of the Dead – a useful handbook of spells for the mummy to recite to make sure he or she travelled safely through the underworld. A map of the underworld was provided, too.

Before the mummy was buried, in a special ceremony, priests used an instrument to open the mummy's mouth so that he or she could eat and drink in the afterlife. Finally, the mummy was laid in a sarcophagus and placed in the tomb with all the goods.

3-second sum-up

The Egyptians mummified pharaohs' bodies and buried them in tombs for the afterlife.

Surprise discovery

Scientists use MRI scans to study mummies. MRI scans make images of the insides of a body. In 2014, scientists at the British Museum, made a gruesome discovery while making an MRI scan of a mummy. The scientists noticed a spatula inside the mummy's skull, obviously left there by a careless embalmer after scooping out the brain.

Mummies were wrapped in bandages, laid in a sarophagus and placed in a tomb with goods for the afterlife.

The embalmers placed amulets in the wrappings to protect the body.

The mummy was wrapped in linen, while a priest read out spells.

A metal blade called an adze was used in the ritual to open the mouth.

Egyptian pictures of the ceremony show the god Anubis holding up the mummy.

All the goods were placed around the coffin, ready to use in the afterlife.

Pyramid building

The Ancient Egyptians had to think of ways to protect their mummies from the heat, wild animals and robbers. Pharaoh Djoser, who lived in about 2650 BCE, came up with the clever idea of hiding his mummy in a vast pyramid.

Pyramids were designed to look like the mound that Ancient Egyptians believed rose from the water at the start of time, where the sun god stood to create the other gods. Djoser's pyramid had step-shaped sides, but most pyramids had smooth sides.

The Great Pyramid at Giza is the tomb of King Khufu. Built around 2589 BCE, it was the largest stone building in the world. It was constructed from more than 2.3 million limestone blocks, each weighing at least 2.5 tonnes (2.8 tons) – more than the average car! It probably took about 20 years to build.

Workers used copper and stone tools to cut the vast blocks of stone needed to build the pyramid, and they may have had levers to move the stones into place. Some experts think they had ramps for raising them, but they had no pulleys to lift the enormous blocks. How did the workers shift them to the high levels of the pyramid? It's still a mystery.

3-second sum-up

The Ancient Egyptians sealed mummies in giant pyramids that took many years to build.

3-minute mission Seven Wonders

The Great Pyramid of Giza is one in a list of Seven Wonders of the ancient world, and the only one that still exists today. Go on the internet and look for images of the other six. What would top your list of modern Wonders?

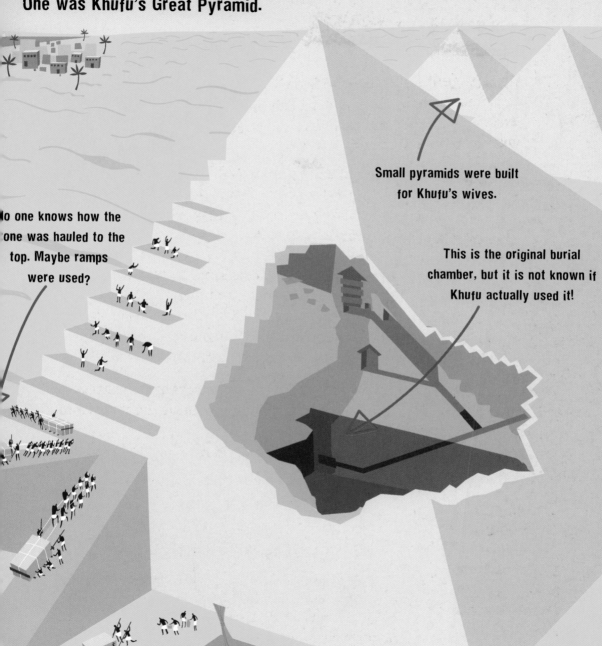

The greatest pyramids were built during the Old Kingdom. One was Khufu's Great Pyramid.

Small pyramids were built for Khufu's wives.

No one knows how the stone was hauled to the top. Maybe ramps were used?

This is the original burial chamber, but it is not known if Khufu actually used it!

A full-size ship was found buried near Khufu's pyramid.

The Valley of the Kings

... in 30 seconds

By 2150 BCE, the great age of pyramid building was over. Pharaohs realized that robbers would break into the pyramids no matter how solidly they were built.

For the next 1,000 years, from around 1500 to 1070 BCE, most pharaohs were buried in the Valley of the Kings, in central Egypt. Instead of pyramids, the pharaohs were buried in elaborate tombs, but no one was supposed to see them.

The pharaohs hid their tombs deep in the hillside, usually down a long corridor with many shafts. At the end was a burial chamber, where the mummy lay in a coffin, along with goods for the afterlife. There were beautiful items such as gold masks, and basic items including furniture.

Cunning robbers still managed to break into the tombs. Then, around 1000 BCE, they were all raided. Several pharaohs robbed the past pharaohs of their treasures to enrich themselves. Amazingly, Tutankhamun's tomb was left untouched until the 20th century.

In 2005, archaeologists discovered tomb goods including pottery and linens in the Valley of Kings, so there must be another well-hidden tomb there somewhere. Perhaps the ancient thieves missed it too...

3-second sum-up

Many pharaohs were buried in complex tombs in the Valley of the Kings.

Finders keepers?

What would do if you found ancient treasure? Would you keep it, sell it for a fortune or take it to a museum? In fact different countries have different rules about treasure finds. For example, in the UK, if you find gold coins on your land you may be able to sell them and keep the money!

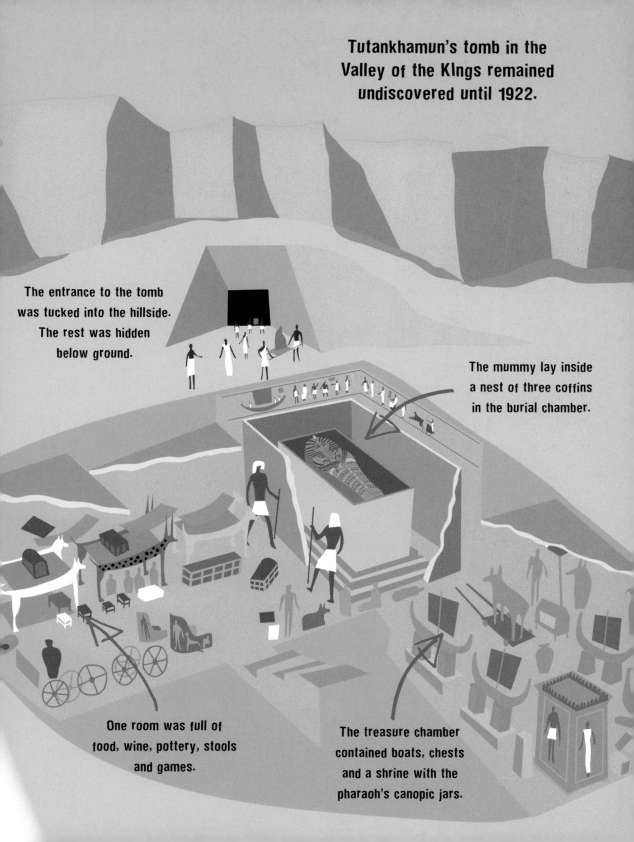

Tutankhamun's tomb in the Valley of the Kings remained undiscovered until 1922.

The entrance to the tomb was tucked into the hillside. The rest was hidden below ground.

The mummy lay inside a nest of three coffins in the burial chamber.

One room was full of food, wine, pottery, stools and games.

The treasure chamber contained boats, chests and a shrine with the pharaoh's canopic jars.

Trading and raiding

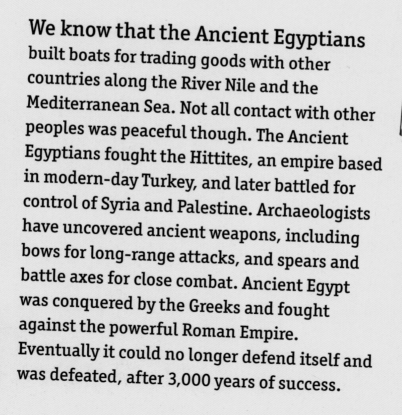

We know that the Ancient Egyptians built boats for trading goods with other countries along the River Nile and the Mediterranean Sea. Not all contact with other peoples was peaceful though. The Ancient Egyptians fought the Hittites, an empire based in modern-day Turkey, and later battled for control of Syria and Palestine. Archaeologists have uncovered ancient weapons, including bows for long-range attacks, and spears and battle axes for close combat. Ancient Egypt was conquered by the Greeks and fought against the powerful Roman Empire. Eventually it could no longer defend itself and was defeated, after 3,000 years of success.

Trading and raiding
Glossary

cargo The goods carried in a boat.

chariot An open vehicle with two wheels, pulled by horses, used in battles.

chariotry The part of the Ancient Egyptian army that fought from horse-drawn chariots.

civilization A state of human society that is very developed and organized.

counter-attack An attack made in response to the attack of an enemy in war.

current The movement of water in the sea or a river.

division A unit of an army, made up of several large groups of soldiers.

downstream The direction in which a river flows.

empire A group of countries or states that are controlled by one ruler or government.

fertile Land where plants grow well.

general The person who led an army in Ancient Egypt.

hieroglyph A picture or symbol of an object that stood for a word or sound in the Ancient Egyptian writing system.

imported Brought in or introduced from another country.

incense A substance that produces a pleasant smell when you burn it, used particularly in religious ceremonies or for healing.

invader An army that enters another country by force to take control of it – this is called an invasion.

ivory A hard yellow-white substance like bone that forms the tusks (long, curved teeth) of elephants.

linen A type of cloth made from the flax plant. The Egyptians used linen to make clothing. We still use linen today.

looting Stealing things when order has broken down, for example, during a war.

official Someone who has a job in the government and can tell people what to do.

papyrus Paper made from the stems of the papyrus plant, used in Ancient Egypt for writing and drawing on.

slingshot In Ancient Egypt, a strap that was fitted over a finger and used as a weapon to fling small stones at an enemy.

surrender In war, to admit that you have been beaten and want to stop fighting.

upstream Along a river, in the opposite direction to the way in which the water flows.

Travel and transport

... in 30 seconds

The Ancient Egyptians had no need to build roads
– why walk when you could float? The River Nile provided the perfect
way to transport goods and people through the country.

From around 4000 BCE, the Egyptians made simple fishing
boats from papyrus reeds, which they rowed with oars or poles.
From Old Kingdom times (see page 12), they built large wooden
cargo ships to transport goods and travel overseas.

Going downstream was easy – the boat drifted with the current.
To go upstream, a sail was raised to catch the wind. Luckily, the
wind was usually blowing in the right direction.

Travelling overland was tough. People trudged along in a caravan
(group), with donkeys carrying their goods. In the 17th century BCE,
invaders from the Middle East, the Hyksos, introduced horses. Now
pharaohs could travel in style, in horse-drawn chariots.

3-second sum-up

The Ancient
Egyptians mostly
travelled by boats
rowed with oars
and made from
papyrus reeds.

3-minute mission Mini boat

You will need: • 20 bendy drinking straws • Duct tape
• String • Scissors

1 With the bendy parts at the top, pinch one end of a straw
and push it into another. Join the other 18 straws in the
same way, making ten extra-long straws.

2 Line up the ten straws in horizontal rows. Wrap duct tape
around the centre, where they join. Bend up the flexible
parts so the boat curves at each end.

3 Pinch together the straws at each end and tie with
string. Wrap tape around the two bendy parts to secure the
shape. Now float your boat!

Boats or walking were the most common methods of travelling. Horses were introduced in the 17th century BCE.

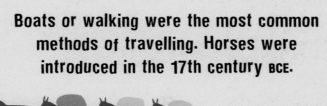

Donkeys were used to carry goods overland.

Light, horse-drawn chariots had four-spoked wheels.

Small boats rowed with oars were perfect for travelling on the Nile.

People used wooden boats with oars and sails to cope with the blustery Mediterranean Sea.

The back oar was used for steering.

A plumbline was used to test the depth of the water.

The market

... in 30 seconds

Every Egyptian town had a busy market where people bought and sold food, clothes, household goods and farm animals.

In major cities such as Memphis and Thebes, you could find a huge variety of delicious foods, including pomegranates, melons, figs, olives, dates and over 30 kinds of bread. Craftspeople sold vases, statues, and carvings in wood, stone, metal and ivory.

The Ancient Egyptians didn't use money, so they used a barter system instead. If you had plenty of ducks but wanted a pair of sandals, you could work out how many ducks you needed to buy the sandals. Traders used a standard weight, called a deben, to work out what an item was worth. For example, a goat was worth 1 deben and a bed cost 2.5 debens. Market officials sorted out any arguments between traders.

The Egyptians traded with other countries, too. They exchanged Egyptian grain, papyrus and linen for precious stones, gold, jewels, woods, incense, spices and oil.

3-second sum-up

The Ancient Egyptians traded at the local market and with other countries.

3-minute mission Swap shop

Work out a barter system for trading things with your friends. For example, you might decide that a packet of mini-felt tips is worth two chocolate bars or that a pack of cards is worth three apples. Make sure everyone is happy with the system before you start.

The Ancient Egyptians traded goods, ranging from livestock to food, at markets.

People could trade food for clothes and other goods.

Goods were weighed to work out their value.

Wine was imported from other countries.

Soldiers and weapons

... in 30 seconds

Before the New Kingdom, armies were formed only when there was a war to fight, and the soldiers went home when it was over.

During the New Kingdom, being a soldier became a career. Boys as young as five were signed up to serve in the army all their lives. But they didn't have to fight until they were 20 – older than in armies today! Others joined as adults.

The pharaoh was the head of the army and he had two generals, for Upper and Lower Egypt. Each army had a navy, a chariotry and an infantry (foot soldiers).

Each chariot was pulled by two fast horses – one soldier drove the chariot while the other fired his arrows at the enemy. Most soldiers were in the infantry. Their most important weapon was the bow and arrow – they could shoot arrows more than 180 m (600 ft). They also fought bloody hand-to-hand battles with axes, daggers and swords.

The pharaoh made good use of his soldiers between wars. They worked in the fields, sowing and harvesting crops, and helped to build pyramids, palaces and temples.

3-second sum-up

Soldiers were armed with a variety of weapons but did not have armour.

Bodybuilding

As part of their training, soldiers lifted heavy sandbags to strengthen their muscles. They learned to fight using knives, spears and sticks, and practised wrestling with other trainee soldiers.

The Ancient Egyptian army had foot soldiers, soldiers on chariots and a navy.

The infantry had axes, daggers and swords. If they were lucky, they had a shield for protection.

An arrow shot from a fast-moving chariot was a deadly weapon.

In sea battles, soldiers fired arrows and slingshots at the enemy ship.

Waging war

... in 30 seconds

Ancient Egypt had few invaders for the first half of its history because enemies struggled to reach it through the desert.

Then, in about 1630 BCE, people called the Hyksos seized control of Egypt. It wasn't all bad though – the Hyksos introduced the horse and chariot, and improved bows and axes, which was very helpful for Egyptian warfare. The Egyptians forced them out 100 years later.

Egypt sometimes started wars, too. In around 1468 BCE, King Thutmose III fought the Canaanites at the Battle of Megiddo. Egypt won the war, and Canaan came under Egypt's control.

In 1275 BCE, Egypt fought the Hittites at the Battle of Kadesh. The Hittites defeated two divisions of the Egyptian army and then, thinking the war was over, they began looting. But two other Egyptian divisions counter-attacked and wiped out the Hittite chariot force. The Hittites didn't give up. They attacked again the following day and many died on both sides. Both the Egyptians and Hittites claimed victory, but in fact it was a draw.

3-second sum-up

The Egyptians fought with the Hyksos, Canaanites and Hittites.

Surprise attack

An Ancient Egyptian story tells how King Thutmose III's general Djehuti invited the Prince of Joppa to meet him near the city of Joppa (modern Jaffa). When the prince arrived, Djehuti knocked him out. Then he hid 200 Egyptian soldiers in large sacks. He sent a message to Joppa that Egypt had surrendered and was sending gifts to the city. But his soldiers were the 'gifts'! Once inside Joppa, the soldiers leapt out of the sacks and conquered the city.

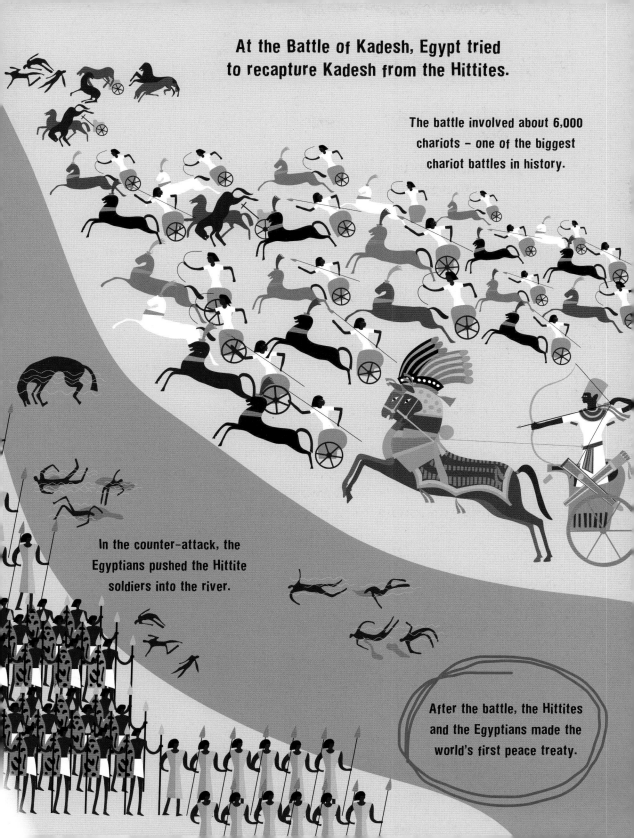

At the Battle of Kadesh, Egypt tried to recapture Kadesh from the Hittites.

The battle involved about 6,000 chariots – one of the biggest chariot battles in history.

In the counter-attack, the Egyptians pushed the Hittite soldiers into the river.

After the battle, the Hittites and the Egyptians made the world's first peace treaty.

The end of Ancient Egypt

... in 30 seconds

All civilizations rise and fall, and eventually the extraordinary 3,000-year-long Ancient Egyptian civilization came to an end. In 332 BCE, the determined young Greek ruler Alexander the Great seized Egypt. When his empire collapsed in 310 BCE, the Greek King Ptolemy I took over. Although the rulers were Greek, Egyptian religion and culture continued.

The Greeks ruled for about 300 years – Cleopatra became the last Greek queen in 51 BCE. By now, the Roman Empire was growing powerful and its rulers had their eyes on Egypt, with its fertile land and rich resources. After Cleopatra died in 30 BCE, Egypt became part of the Roman Empire.

The Ancient Egyptian religion declined and Christianity took root instead. People no longer wrote in hieroglyphs and the Egyptian language changed to become similar to Greek. After the Arab invasion of 640 CE, the Egyptian language disappeared, too. Through the Bible, people remembered Ancient Egypt, but the details of its long and complex history were buried.

3-second sum-up

The Roman Empire took over Egypt in 30 BCE, and Ancient Egyptian culture died out.

The Rosetta Stone

After Ancient Egypt fell, people forgot how to read hieroglyphs. Then, in 1799, a broken Ancient Egyptian stone was discovered with writing on it. At first no one knew what it said, but eventually scholars managed to decode the writing as it had both Ancient Greek and hieroglyphs. At last hieroglyphic texts could be translated, allowing us to find out all about the great Ancient Egyptian civilization.

Mediterranean Sea

From 332 BCE, the Ancient Egyptian civilization went into decline.

In 332 BCE Egypt became part of Alexander the Great's huge Greek empire.

River Nile

In 51 BCE Cleopatra became the last Greek queen. It is said she killed herself with snake poison.

In 30 BCE the Roman leader Octavian defeated Cleopatra and Egypt became part of the Roman Empire.

Discover more

FICTION BOOKS

Ancient Egypt: Tales of Gods and Pharaohs by Marcia Williams
Walker, 2012

Tales of Ancient Egypt by Roger Lancelyn Green and Michael Rosen
Puffin Classics, 2011

The Egypt Game by Zilpha Keatley Snyder
Atheneum/Simon & Schuster, 2009

The Magic and the Mummy (Egyptian Tales) by Terry Deary
A&C Black, 2004

The Time-travelling Cat and the Egyptian Goddess by Julia Jarman
Andersen, 2006

*Treasury of Egyptian Mythology: Classic Stories of Gods, Goddesses,
Monsters & Mortals* by Donna Jo Napoli
National Geographic Kids, 2013

NON-FICTION BOOKS

Ancient Egypt (100 Facts) by Jane Walker
Miles Kelly Publishing, 2006

Ancient Egypt (Eyewitness) by Dorling Kindersley
Dorling Kindersley, 2014

Awful Egyptians (Horrible Histories) by Terry Deary
Scholastic, 2013

Egypt (See Inside) by Rob Lloyd Jones
Usborne Publishing, 2007

Everything Ancient Egypt: Dig into a Treasure Trove of Facts, Photos and Fun
by Crispin Boyer
National Geographic Kids, 2012

If I Were a Kid in Ancient Egypt by Cobblestone Publishing
Cobblestone Publishing, 2007

ACTIVITY BOOKS

Ancient Egypt (Eyewitness Project Books) by Dorling Kindersley
Dorling Kindersley, 2009

Ancient Egypt Scratch and Sketch by Suzanne Beilenson
Peter Pauper Press, 2006

Egyptian Things to Make and Do (Usborne Activities) by Emily Bone
Usborne Publishing, 2011

DVDs – suitable for all ages

Ancient Egypt (Go Entertain, 2007)

Ancient Egypt Unearthed (Discovery, 2009)

Awesome Egyptians (Horrible Histories) (Delta Music, 2005)

Discovery Channel Ancient Egypt (Discovery Channel, 2012)

National Geographic: Mysteries Of Egypt (CAV Distribution, 2010)

WEB SITES

Ancient Egypt Online
http://ancientegyptonline.org/aeoHTML/index.html
Facts, photos and an interactive map of Ancient Egypt.

National Geographic Kids
http://www.ngkids.co.uk/did-you-know/Ten-Facts-about-Ancient-Egypt
Videos, photos and facts about Ancient Egypt.

Primary Homework Help: Ancient Egypt
http://primaryhomeworkhelp.co.uk/egypt/activities.htm
Facts and interactive activities about Ancient Egypt.

The British Museum
http://www.ancientegypt.co.uk/menu.html
Facts, stories and games for children as well as teachers' pages
and class worksheets.

Index